Music
Scene

The History of Modern Music

Matt Anniss

FRANKLIN WATTS
LONDON•SYDNEY

First published 2012 by Franklin Watts
338 Euston Road
London NW1 3BH

Franklin Watts Australia
Level 17/207 Kent Street
Sydney, NSW 2000

Produced by Calcium, www.calciumcreative.co.uk

A CIP catalogue record for this book is available from
the British Library.

ISBN 978 1 4451 1389 0

Dewey classification: 781.6'4'09

Printed in China

Franklin Watts is a division of Hachette Children's Books,
an Hachette UK company
www.hachette.co.uk

Acknowledgements:
The publisher would like to thank the following for permission to
reproduce photographs: Corbis: Sunset Boulevard 19t; Dreamstime:
Mira Agron 38, Rui Dias Aidos 18, Larisa Chernisheva 35br, Howsat
17, Imagecollect 41, Joyfull 35t, Pressureua 42, Stormarn 15t; Getty
Images: Redferns 13; iStockphoto: EdStock2 29bl, D Withers 14;
Library of Congress: Herman Hiller 12t, Warren K Leffler 12bl, Metro-
Goldwyn-Mayer Inc 6, United Press International 10; Rex Features: 28,
Kevin Cole 8, Everett Collection 36, Terry O'Neill 9, Sheila Rock 22t,
Richard Young 22b, 27; Shutterstock: Admedia 32t, Anthony Correia
39b, Excellent backgrounds 33, Andrija Kovac 19b, Aija Lehtonen 23,
Northfoto 25tl, 34, 43b, Oliveromg 5, 40, Ferenc Szelepcsenyi 21b, Jeff
Thrower cover; Spotify: 43tr; Wikipedia: 2xUeL 26, A l'origine 31, Joel
Brodksy/Electra Records 15br, Bryan Coastales 16, Will Fresch 37b,
Simon Green 30-31, Joho34 25r, Klau Klettner/Hydra Records 7, Lola's
Big Adventure! 37r, Wolfgang Moroder 24, Masao Nakagami 32bl,
Notorious TF 21tr, Scootie 30b, Squelle 29tr, Deborah Wilbanks 39l.

Every attempt has been made to clear copyright. Should there be any
inadvertent omission please apply to the publisher for rectification.

CONTENTS

CHAPTER ONE

THE BIRTH OF MODERN MUSIC

At the end of World War Two in 1945, few would have believed that within ten years a musical revolution would take place in the USA. In the mid 1950s, a new form of music took the world by storm and set in motion 60 years of musical adventure and experimentation. This new music was rock and roll.

Divided nation

In the years following World War Two, the USA was still a nation divided by strict race laws. Black people in the country did not have the same freedoms as white people and were considered by the racist system as second-class citizens. Because of this, the musical sounds and traditions of the country's black and white populations were kept separate.

Joining together

In the early 1950s, white musicians began to make music that was heavily influenced by traditionally black styles such as rhythm and blues and jazz. The first music to fuse black and white music styles was rockabilly. This was a combination of the heavy beats and rhythms of blues, folk and country music influences.

Enter Elvis

In 1954, Elvis Presley (right), the former trucker from Memphis, Tennessee, had a worldwide hit with a rockabilly song called That's Alright Mama. Teenagers loved the song and Elvis quickly became the headline star of a worldwide rock and roll revolution.

Rock Around the Clock

Rock and roll was slightly different to rockabilly. It featured electric instruments and was similar to rhythm and blues. It was first made popular by Bill Haley and the Comets, whose 1955 song *Rock Around the Clock* became a worldwide hit.

The goss

Although Rock Around the Clock and That's Alright Mama were huge hits, many music historians think that Little Richard's Tutti Frutti was the song that really kick-started rock and roll. Recorded and released in 1955, its simple energy and heavy sound inspired a whole new generation of would-be stars.

Bill Haley's fun songs helped to make rock and roll a worldwide phenomenon in the 1950s.

Teenage kicks

There were two things about rock and roll that made it attractive to teenagers. Firstly, it was music they could dance to. Secondly, their parents hated it! The older generation couldn't understand the music's raw power and loud chords. This just made teenagers love rock and roll even more. It was something that was 'theirs' and separated them from their parents.

Revolution in sound

For the first time ever, buying, playing and listening to music became an essential part of being a teenager. Rock and roll changed the way teenagers dressed, spoke and how they spent their spare time. Sales of vinyl records soared and organised rock and roll dances, often called 'record hops', became the place to be seen. In future, nothing would be the same again. Today's bands might not make rock and roll, but without these 1950s pioneers we would have no rock music at all today.

THE BRITISH ARE COMING

American rock and roll ruled in the late 1950s, but by the mid 1960s the world was dancing to different sounds. They came from the UK, and most specifically the cities of Liverpool and Manchester.

The biggest rock and pop stars of the 1960s were followed by fanatical groups of screaming teenage fans.

A new sound

Rock and roll had a big impact on many British teenagers. But it was a British version of rock and roll called 'skiffle' that made the biggest impact. Skiffle was played with acoustic instruments rather than electric ones, and made popular by the singer Lonnie Donegan. Inspired by skiffle and Elvis, many teenagers formed their own bands.

A new beat

By the early 1960s, many skiffle bands had 'gone electric' and replaced their homemade music-making equipment with instruments. These young bands began to make a form of pop music that was influenced by rock and roll, but had a very British sound. It was called 'beat music'. Nowhere was beat music more popular than in Liverpool.

From The Cavern to the charts

The beat music scene in Liverpool was based around a music venue called The Cavern Club. It was here that many local bands first played and where they perfected their sound.

The goss

One of the most successful Merseybeat bands of the early 1960s was Gerry and the Pacemakers. They set a record when their first three singles reached number one in the British charts. No one had ever done that before — not even The Beatles!

One of these bands, The Beatles, rose up the British charts in 1964. Record labels quickly rushed to sign more groups from Liverpool and soon these groups, nicknamed 'Merseybeat bands' ruled the charts.

The invasion begins

It wasn't long before American teenagers began to get a taste for British beat music. In 1964, The Beatles made their first trip to the USA. After appearing on a popular television chat show, they were headline news. Their concerts sold out and their music sold in record-breaking time. In one week in April 1964, The Beatles held the top five positions on the Billboard Top 100 chart.

Blues clues

British pop music at the time was also greatly influenced by the heavier sound of American rhythm and blues. In London, a homegrown blues scene developed. Bands such as The Rolling Stones, The Kinks, and The Who gave audiences a sound that was far rougher than the clean-cut pop created by the Merseybeat bands. It wasn't long before these bands had made their mark in the USA and led the way to a decade of dominance by British rock that lasted into the early 1970s. Even recent bands such as Oasis, Blur, and The Killers owe a debt to British pop of the 1960s.

Rule Britannia

Following The Beatles, many other British bands were successful in the USA. The American media called this 'The British Invasion'. Alongside The Beatles, the USA also fell in love with The Dave Clark Five, Freddie and the Dreamers, and Herman's Hermits.

The Rolling Stones are still making records today, over 50 years after recording their first-ever song.

9

The Beatles

The Beatles are the most successful band ever. During the 1960s, John Lennon, Paul McCartney, Ringo Starr and George Harrison recorded some of the best-known music of the time. They were the first pop band to achieve worldwide fame.

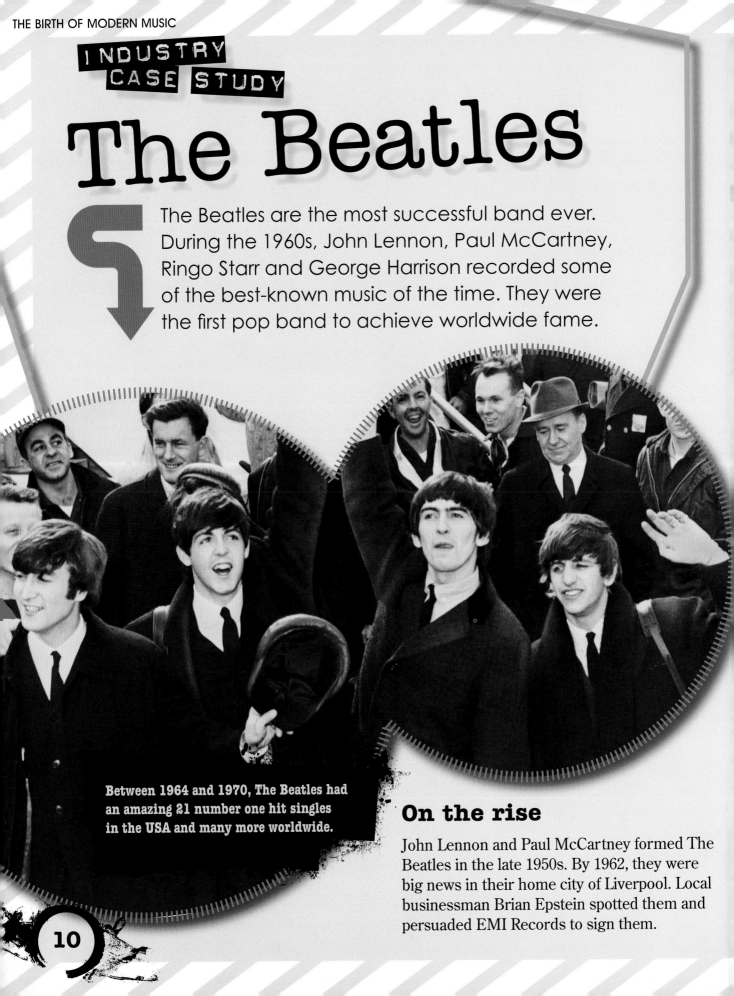

Between 1964 and 1970, The Beatles had an amazing 21 number one hit singles in the USA and many more worldwide.

On the rise

John Lennon and Paul McCartney formed The Beatles in the late 1950s. By 1962, they were big news in their home city of Liverpool. Local businessman Brian Epstein spotted them and persuaded EMI Records to sign them.

Beatlemania

Thanks to a clean-cut image and catchy pop songs in their own unique Merseybeat style, The Beatles became international stars in 1964. 'Beatlemania' spread and the band couldn't go anywhere without being followed by crowds of screaming fans.

Bright stars

During 1964 and 1965, The Beatles were probably the most famous people on the planet. They starred in two successful films, *A Hard Day's Night* and *Help!*, and spent most of their time touring the world. They played concerts in huge sports stadiums, playing their hit singles to crowds of teenage girls.

Studio time

The Beatles soon tired of their fame and decided to stop touring in 1966. Instead, they focused on making music in the recording studio. Musically, they had already started experimenting with the 1965 album *Rubber Soul*, but the albums that followed in 1966 and 1967 revolutionised the music industry.

New sounds

With the aid of producer George Martin and almost unlimited studio time, The Beatles were able to experiment with new sounds and recording techniques.

Making it big

After The Beatles recorded their second single in London's Abbey Road studios, George Martin famously said "Congratulations gentlemen, you've just made your first number one record". He was proved right as Please Please Me rocketed to the top of the British charts.

Their 1966 album *Revolver* featured songs recorded with violins and cellos, people playing traditional Indian instruments and a soul-style horn section. Most revolutionary was a song called *Tomorrow Never Knows*, which used the sort of cutting-edge tape editing and looping techniques that had rarely been heard before.

Everything changes

Revolver and its follow-up *Sgt. Pepper's Lonely Hearts Club Band* had a huge impact. They showed not only the limitless potential of rock and pop music, but also what could be achieved in the recording studio. In the following years, albums became works of art – not just collections of songs.

TIMELINE: The Beatles

1957: Paul McCartney joins John Lennon's skiffle group, The Quarrymen
1960: The Quarrymen change their name to The Beatles
1962: *Love Me Do* single hits UK Top 20
1963: *Please Please Me* tops album chart

1964: Beatlemania sweeps the USA
1966: *Revolver* album is released
1967: *Sgt. Pepper's Lonely Hearts Club Band* album is released
1970: The Beatles final album, *Let It Be*, is released and the group splits up

SOUL POWER

In the 1950s, white Americans reinvented black forms of music. In the 1960s, black performers hit the pop charts with a style that crossed over into the mainstream – soul.

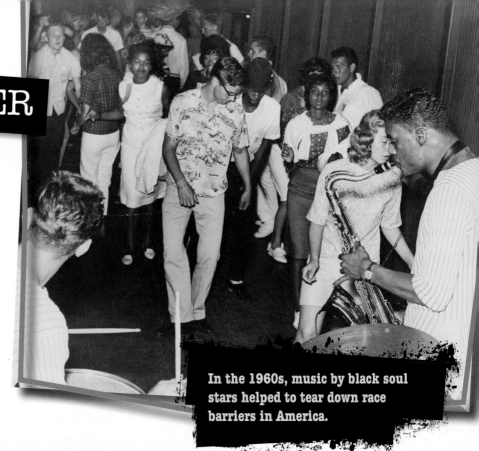

In the 1960s, music by black soul stars helped to tear down race barriers in America.

The rise of soul music in the 1960s helped to spur on black Americans in their struggle for equal rights.

Difficult times

The USA in the 1960s was a country still full of racial problems, with laws that meant black people were not allowed basic human rights. Even in these hard times, some black performers were able to become successful pop stars. Their success paved the way for black performers to dominate the global music scene.

Got to have soul

Soul music first developed in the late 1950s in the northern US cities of Chicago and Detroit. Here, singers and musicians had been raised on gospel singing in church. They used the skills they'd learned to develop a soulful version of rhythm and blues, which was popular in black communities at the time. The first soul singer to hit the big time was Ray Charles, who had many hit singles in the late 1950s.

Motown begins

In 1959, a Detroit songwriter-turned-businessman called Berry Gordy decided to open two record labels called Tamla and Motown in a house that Gordy called Hitsville USA. Today, Hitsville USA is a museum.

Motown sounds

Many people believe that Berry Gordy, owner of the Tamla and Motown record labels, did the most to make soul music popular. Gordy got together with a group of great local songwriters and musicians and set out to make pop hits. He signed up record producer Norman Whitfield and a talented songwriting team called Holland-Dozier-Holland. Between them, they were able to create the Motown trademark sound that both white and black teenagers loved. Many Motown Records artists made it to the top of the Billboard Top 100 pop charts as a result.

Motown stars

In the early 1960s, Motown Records had hits from artists such as Diana Ross and the Supremes, Martha and the Vandellas, Smokey Robinson and the Miracles, The Temptations, Marvin Gaye, and Tammy Tyrell. All became worldwide stars, as the Motown sound became popular in the UK, Europe and Australia.

Diana Ross and the Supremes were the first all-black girl group to conquer the American charts.

The goss

The first Motown Records single to hit number one in the USA was The Marvelettes' Please Mister Postman. It reached the top of the charts in 1961 and was later covered by The Beatles.

Motown forever

The 60s soul sound of the Motown and Tamla labels continues to be popular to this day, and many current R&B and pop stars have been influenced by this period. Cee Lo Green, Duffy, and Mayer Hawthorne have all forged careers on the back of records that sound like old Motown hits. Even some big R&B records such as Beyoncé's *Crazy in Love* contain elements of long forgotten 1960s soul records.

CHANGING TIMES

The late 1960s was a difficult time. World events such as the Vietnam War and the assassination of would-be president Robert Kennedy, plus social changes such as the hippy movement and the black civil rights movement, had a big effect on the music of the era.

Speaking out

In the mid to late 1960s, an alternative (or underground) music movement was growing in both the UK and the USA. In the US, folk rock musicians such as Bob Dylan, Leonard Cohen, and Simon and Garfunkel expressed their thoughts on social and political issues through their music.

War cry

Many musicians were inspired to create music that spoke about the Vietnam War. The conflict had been ongoing since the early 1960s, but became big news when American soldiers were sent to the country in 1965. Many alternative musicians felt strongly that the Vietnam War was wrong and that the United States shouldn't be involved.

Flower power

A number of protest singers became part of an underground music and lifestyle scene in San Francisco, California, that became known as the 'hippy movement'. Hippies believed in peace, love and individual freedom. Their message spread around the world. Many underground musicians, and even famous ones such as The Beatles, shared their beliefs and included hippy ideals in the music that they made.

Psychedelia

In the late 1960s, many musicians experimented with taking dangerous, mind-altering drugs such as LSD. These drugs ruined many lives by seriously damaging people's mental and physical health, but they also inspired some bands to make strange and exciting new rock, soul and pop music. This music was said to be psychedelic. As a result, psychedelic rock was one of the biggest musical forms of the period.

The Beatles changed pop music forever with their psychedelic album *Sgt. Pepper's Lonely Hearts Club Band.*

The goss

Illegal drugs have destroyed the lives of a number of underground rock stars over the years. In 1970, American guitarist Jimi Hendrix (left) died of a drugs overdose at the age of 28. He was one of the brightest stars of underground music.

60s to noughties

In 2011, a new wave of folk rock bands began to climb up the charts. Acts such as Bon Iver, Mumford and Sons, and Bellowhead owe much to the 1970s sound of Bob Dylan and Simon and Garfunkel. Meanwhile, some strains of electronic music such as ambient and trance borrow elements from psychedelic music. Even heavy rockers such as Red Hot Chili Peppers can trace their roots back to 1960s funk-rock!

Alternative sounds

On both sides of the Atlantic, teenagers and young people were beginning to buy more music influenced by underground culture. In universities and colleges, students gathered to listen to bands such as The Doors and The Grateful Dead, who were known as alternative rockers. Meanwhile, already successful rock and pop acts such as The Beatles, The Who, and The Beach Boys began to make records inspired by the psychedelic music that was taking over.

Underground goes overground

By the end of the 1960s, alternative or 'progressive' rock music had become one of the best-selling styles in the world. What was once thought of as underground music had become mainstream. It set a trend. In future, many underground styles of music crossed over into the pop charts.

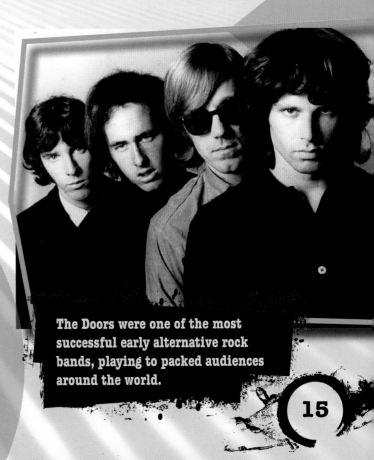

The Doors were one of the most successful early alternative rock bands, playing to packed audiences around the world.

CHAPTER TWO

EVERYTHING CHANGES

Music festivals occur each summer, with acts as diverse as Beyoncé, Jay-Z, U2, Coldplay, and Radiohead playing headline sets at massive events all around the world. It hasn't always been this way – until 1967, there were no rock and pop festivals at all.

Crowds flocked to see Jefferson Airplane at the Fantasy Fair and Magic Mountain Festival.

Fantasy festival

All modern music festivals can trace their beginnings back to an event in San Francisco, California, called the Fantasy Fair and Magic Mountain Festival. Headlined by Canned Heat, Captain Beefheart, and The Byrds, the festival took place over two days in June 1967. It marked the beginning of what has become known as rock music's 'Summer of Love'.

The word spreads

The following year, more music festivals began to spring up around the world. In the USA, two weekend-long events were held at a race track in Florida called the Miami Pop Festival. Meanwhile, over in the UK, 10,000 people travelled to a small island off the south coast of the UK for the first ever Isle of Wight Festival, which has since become one of the world's most popular festivals.

Trailblazers

While these festivals paved the way for the future, there were a number of events in 1969 that really put the rock festival on the map. Perhaps the most famous of all these festivals was Woodstock, a non-stop, three-day event that was held in New York State, USA.

Legendary Woodstock

Woodstock has become legendary for a number of reasons, not least stand-out performances from headliners such as Jefferson Airplane, Joan Baez, Sly and the Family Stone, and The Who. It is estimated that over 500,000 people attended the Woodstock festival, making it one of the biggest music festivals ever – even to date, this is one of the largest festival attendances.

The goss

One of the most talked about performances in the history of rock music took place at the Woodstock festival in 1969. It came from guitarist Jimi Hendrix, who wowed festival-goers with a solo version of the American national anthem, Star Spangled Banner. It has become one of rock music's most iconic moments.

Watching Dylan

Over in the UK, two other festivals in 1969 made a huge impact. One was the second Isle of Wight Festival, which attracted a record 150,000 people to see Bob Dylan play. It was the singer-songwriter's first live appearance since he had been hurt in a motorbike accident in 1968. The pull of Dylan's appearance was such that even members of The Beatles and The Rolling Stones turned up to watch the legendary performer.

Bath blues

There was another festival that summer that was hugely important. Held in the city of Bath, the Bath Festival of Blues featured appearances from rhythm and blues bands such as Fleetwood Mac and John Mayall and the Bluesbreakers. More importantly, it inspired a farmer called Michael Eavis to host his own music festival – Glastonbury. Today, Glastonbury is a huge music event that has a worldwide audience.

Glastonbury begins

Michael Eavis hosted the first Glastonbury festival on his farm in Pilton, Somerset, UK, in September 1970. Tickets cost £1 and 1,500 people attended. The first band to play at the festival was a local group called Stackridge.

The Arcadia stage was one of 59 stages at the Glastonbury Festival of 2011.

17

RISE OF DISCO

During the 1970s, a new form of music took nightclubs by storm – disco. Its rise led to a boom in nightclubs and the birth of the club DJ. In the process, dance music culture was born.

Disco funk

Disco started to become a style of music in its own right in the mid 1970s. Musicians began to make longer soul and funk tracks to appeal to nightclub dancers. It wasn't long before a strong disco sound developed, featuring heavy drum beats, strings, funky basslines and soulful vocals.

The effects of disco music on fashion in the 1970s can still be felt today.

Rise of the DJ

In the clubs of New York City, groundbreaking DJs such as Francis Grasso, Nicky Siano, and Walter Gibbons realised that they could create a seamless performance by matching the drum beats in two different records and mixing them together. Almost overnight, the DJ as we know it was created.

Disco spreads

In the mid to late 1970s, disco spread beyond the underground nightclubs of New York City and Philadelphia. Clubs such as Studio 54 in New York, and hit records from artists such as Donna Summer, Chic, The Jacksons, and The Bee Gees, made disco a big hit worldwide and the number of people regularly going to nightclubs soared.

The goss

One of the world's longest-running disco events is called The Loft. These gigs were first held in the New York attic apartment of a music fan called David Mancuso in 1970. They are still going to this day, with similar events held in London and Tokyo, Japan.

Night fever

Disco hit the big screen in 1977 with the popular film *Saturday Night Fever*. This story about a New York teenager who escapes his troubles by becoming a champion disco dancer caught the imagination of audiences

across the world. The soundtrack album, featuring songs by The Bee Gees and The Trammps, is one of the biggest-selling albums of all time.

Big comeback

The popularity of disco faded at the end of the 1970s, but by then both DJing and nightclub culture had become widespread. In recent years, 1970s disco has become very popular once more, as DJs and musicians such as Madonna, Daft Punk, and Lady Gaga rediscover dance music.

John Travolta's dancing in *Saturday Night Fever* turned the world on to disco music.

Remix culture

Today, many pop songs have extra-long versions designed to appeal to dancers in nightclubs. These are known as 'remixes' and were first created in the disco era by a man named Tom Moulton. He made remixes especially for DJs, pressing them onto vinyl records in very small quantities. They were so popular that, in 1976, record labels began to release special 12-inch singles.

Disco DJs helped to turn playing records in clubs into the art form it is today.

The Sugarhill Gang

New York in the 1970s was alive with new musical developments. Alongside disco, the city also created one of the biggest music styles of the twentieth century – hip-hop. This pioneering work paved the way for current rap superstars such as Eminem, 50 Cent and Lil' Wayne.

Kool beginnings

On 11 August 1973, a party took place at a community centre in the Bronx neighbourhood of New York City. The DJ for the night was a Jamaican-born music fan called Kool Herc. He amazed dancers by using two copies of the same record on two turntables to extend the song's heavy drum patterns. As he did this, he talked, or rapped, over the records on a microphone.

Bronx block parties

Soon, many other local DJs were copying Kool Herc's extended drum breaks at illegal outdoor block parties all over the Bronx. One DJ, Grandmaster Flash, went even further by refining 'quick mix' mixing and inventing scratching – quickly moving a record backwards and forwards by hand to create a variety of noises.

TIMELINE: The birth of hip-hop

1973: DJ Kool Herc uses two records to extend sections of dance records

1976: DJ Grandmaster Flash unveils his 'quick mix theory'

1977: Grandmaster Flash forms The Furious Five, the first established

1978: Lovebug Starski becomes the first in-house rapper at the Disco Fever club in the Bronx

1979: The Sugarhill Gang records and releases *Rapper's Delight*

1979: Grandmaster Flash and the Furious Five release their *Superrappin'* single

Break dance beats

In the late 1970s, the roles of the DJ and the microphone man separated. DJs concentrated on creating a good atmosphere for local dance fans known as 'break dancers' while MCs, or rappers, spoke in rhyme over the music.

Good times

In the early days of hip-hop, there was no single style of music used by DJs and rappers. DJs played a variety of music, focusing on the heavy drum breaks found in rock, disco, soul, funk, Latin and pop.

Along with DJ Kool Herc, Grandmaster Flash invented turntable techniques that are still used by today's hip-hop DJs.

Modern rappers such as Xzibit owe their livelihoods to New York's 1970s hip-hop pioneers.

History maker

What hip-hop needed to go global was a hit record. That came in 1979. New York businesswoman Sylvia Robinson heard hip-hop DJs and rappers at a party in New York and decided the time was right to record a rap record. She asked her recording studio's house band to record a backing track based on the groove from Chic's *Good Times*. She then asked three New Jersey teenagers to add their own raps.

Rap attack

Credited to The Sugarhill Gang, *Rapper's Delight* was released on 9 November 1979. The 15-minute rap record quickly became a massive smash worldwide, reaching the Top 10 in the UK, Germany, Canada, France, and Australia. In the months and years to come, more hip-hop records were released, and by the late 1980s rap music had become a global force.

ANGRY SOUNDS

During the 1970s, many teenagers in the USA and the UK turned their back on mainstream rock and pop music. Angry at the world around them, they created their own music called punk.

The Ramones blazed a trail by helping to invent an angry new form of rock music called punk.

Trouble brewing

At this time, mainstream music was a mix of glam rock, over-the-top progressive rock, slick soul and goodtime disco. Many teenagers felt that this didn't fit in with their day-to-day lives. All they saw were fewer jobs for school leavers and mass strikes by workers demanding better pay. They were angry about what was happening around them and needed a release.

Cult heroes

Like many teenagers before them, young people turned to music. They began to make loud, simple, angry rock and roll music. Two bands in New York led the way – The New York Dolls and The Ramones. These groups built up a cult following on both sides of the Atlantic and headed a new style called punk rock.

Punk fever spreads

It wasn't long before punk's influence spread to the UK. Punk scenes grew up in cities such as London, Manchester, Birmingham and Sheffield. Led by bands such as The Clash, The Damned, and The Sex Pistols, punk's popularity in the UK quickly grew during 1976.

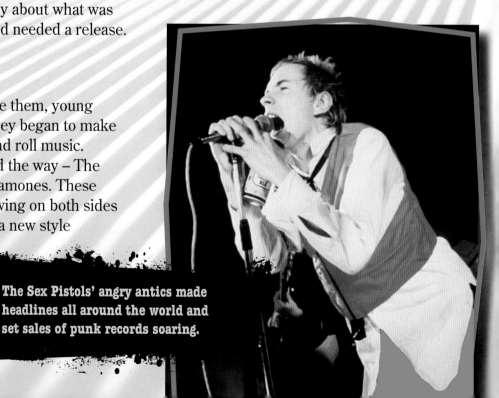

The Sex Pistols' angry antics made headlines all around the world and set sales of punk records soaring.

The goss

In December 1976, The Sex Pistols sparked outrage in British newspapers following a live television interview. During the interview, guitarist Steve Jones repeatedly swore at host Bill Grundy. The shocking incident brought punk rock to wider public attention for the first time.

Anarchy in the UK

The UK's troubled summer of 1977 was filled with strikes and protests. At the same time, the punk rock movement represented the gap between teenagers, their parents and 'the establishment' – namely the police and politicians. The attitude of punk rockers and their simple-but-effective music inspired many British teenagers to form their own bands.

The birth of 'indie'

Punk died out in the early 1980s, but its independent attitude lived on through independent rock and pop bands and record labels. They created the 'indie' scene of today. Punk itself has been reinvented in recent years by 'nu punk' and 'skate punk' bands such as Green Day and Blink-182.

Punk's legacy

1970s punk music is important because it founded the idea of the independent record label. Many 1970s punk artists rejected big deals with major record labels and instead made and released music themselves. This is something many bands still do today, distributing their music using popular websites and online services such as iTunes, SoundCloud, and Bandcamp.

Thanks to the success of Blink-182, Green Day, and The Offspring, punk is still hugely popular today.

CHAPTER THREE

RISE OF THE MACHINES

Ever since the launch of the electric guitar in the 1950s, developments in technology have influenced the way people make and play music. In the late 1970s and early 1980s, new types of electronic instruments changed music forever.

Electronic movement

The first electronic synthesisers (keyboard-like instruments capable of creating futuristic sounds) appeared in the late 1960s. However, it wasn't until the end of the 1970s that they began to be widely used by musicians. At first, they were very expensive and hard to use. It was only when they became cheaper and more user-friendly that their popularity increased.

Kraftwerk

The pioneers of electronic music were a German pop band called Kraftwerk. During the 1970s, they released a series of albums made entirely of electronic sounds. Unlike most pop bands, Kraftwerk used synthesisers and early electronic drum machines rather than traditional instruments such as guitars.

The goss

Kraftwerk had a huge effect on American hip-hop DJ and musician Afrika Bambaataa. He based his hip-hop hit Planet Rock on sections of the Kraftwerk tracks Numbers and Trans Europe Express.

German producer Giorgio Moroder reinvented disco with Donna Summer's *I Feel Love* – a record made using only synthesisers.

In the 1980s, synth-pop bands such as the Pet Shop Boys (pictured) became huge stars around the world.

Computers and music

Synthesisers became more powerful in the early 1980s. During this period, many big recording studios offered musicians the chance to use early music computers such as the Fairlight CMI and Synclavier. These cutting-edge instruments were very expensive and beyond the reach of most musicians. Those who could afford them, used them to make some of the biggest-selling pop records of the time. Prince, R.E.M., U2, Madonna, Fleetwood Mac, and Hall and Oates were all regular users of the Fairlight CMI.

New bands, new sounds

The futuristic sounds of Kraftwerk inspired many young musicians, particularly those in Sheffield, UK. Here, bands such as The Human League and Cabaret Voltaire began to make bleak electronic music using synthesisers they'd built themselves. These bands later had hits in the charts with a brand new style called 'synth-pop'.

The influential Fairlight CMI bridged the gap between analogue synthesisers and digital computers.

Drum breakthroughs

In 1980, an electronics company called Roland released a drum machine called the TR-808. It proved to be one of the musical breakthroughs of the 1980s. More affordable than previous drum machines, it was used by hip-hop producers to create a new sound called Electro. It was also used by dance music producers, disco musicians and synth-pop bands.

Massive changes

Today, a whole new generation of synth-pop and indie-dance bands such as Friendly Fires, Florence and the Machine, and Justice are gaining inspiration from 1980s synthesiser sounds. Many huge pop records by artists such as Lady Gaga also use electronic keyboard sounds.

25

MARRS

In 1987, a brand new electronic instrument called the digital sampler was first heard in popular music. A British band called MARRS used it to create a groundbreaking pop hit called *Pump Up the Volume*. In doing so, they helped to change the way music was made forever.

Small sample

The first digital samplers appeared in the early 1980s. To begin with, few people saw the potential of these machines. They allowed musicians to record, or 'sample', small sections of other people's records, change them and re-use them in their own records.

Cutting up songs

The digital sampler was revolutionary because it meant that new music could be created using bits of previously recorded songs. Japanese electronics manufacturer Akai created its first digital samplers around 1985. Within two years, the process of 'sampling' other people's records blew the industry apart.

Justified art

One of the first bands to hook into the potential of the digital sampler was The Justified Ancients of Mu Mu, who later became the successful dance-pop band The KLF. They created an entire album based around samples of other people's records entitled *1987*.

Digital samplers such as this 1980s model by E-mu Systems allowed people with no musical training to make their own tracks.

Going to court

The Justified Ancients of Mu Mu's *1987* was hailed by music critics as a dramatic step forward. The people whose records had been 'sampled' disagreed. Pop group Abba sued them, forcing the band to withdraw the record from shops. It was the first of many legal battles over music samples.

Sample magic

The MARRS song, *Pump Up the Volume*, became one of the most influential tracks in the UK and USA in the 1980s. It was the first successful hit single to be made almost entirely out of samples of other people's music. It used around 30 different samples from hip-hop, disco, Indian, funk, and dance records.

Copyright issues

The impact of *Pump Up the Volume* was almost instant. It dominated clubs and rocketed to the higher reaches of the British and American charts. A number of artists whose music had been sampled, including producers Stock, Aitken and Waterman and James Brown, sued the band's record label 4AD for copyright infringement. MARRS were forced to hand over a portion of the money they earned from the record's success to the people whose music they'd sampled.

The flood

The success of *Pump Up the Volume* paved the way for the use of sampling in popular music. In the months and years that followed, many pop, dance and hip-hop producers used digital samplers

Public Enemy

MARRS weren't the only band to see the potential of using a digital sampler to make new records. Hip-hop band Public Enemy made almost all of their music out of samples, adding their own raps over the top. Their hits Rebel Without a Pause and Don't Believe the Hype used sampled sounds, beats and riffs.

to help them make new tracks. This type of sampling allowed people with no musical training to make music. It was the first step towards today's musical culture.

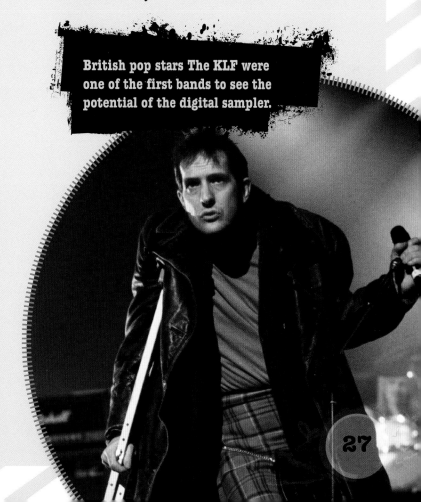

British pop stars The KLF were one of the first bands to see the potential of the digital sampler.

MUSIC MESSAGES

Music with a message didn't end with the fall of punk in 1979. Throughout the 1980s, rock and pop bands used music as a tool to talk about issues affecting their lives. They even used it to raise money for charity.

Bob Geldof was so shocked by the plight of starving African children that he put on a charity concert that raised £20 million.

Times are tough

The 1980s were a tough time in the USA and the UK where youth unemployment was high and the gap between the rich and poor was growing. Tensions between global superpowers the USA and the Soviet Union (now Russia) meant that nuclear war was a very real threat.

Political points

Just as they had in the 1960s and the late 1970s, many musicians responded to the difficulties about the world around them through music. From the 'spooky' pop of The Specials' *Ghost Town*, which was inspired by street riots, to Simply Red's *Money's Too Tight to Mention*, many successful songs had a political message.

Charity records

In 1984, people across the world were horrified by images of starving Africans that started appearing on television news reports. Many people wanted to do something

about it and started raising money for charities working in Africa.

Two musicians decided they'd try to make a difference. Bob Geldof and Midge Ure wanted to get other famous singers to help them make a record that could raise money for famine relief in Africa. That record was *Do They Know It's Christmas?*, credited to Band Aid.

Fight for your rights

The late 1980s saw a rise in hip-hop records that sought to educate American teenagers about the plight of black people in poor areas of cities. Public Enemy frontman Chuck D saw his music as a way of educating people about both black history and issues affecting the lives of millions of black Americans.

Changing the world

Do They Know It's Christmas? featured many of the biggest stars of the time, including members of bands such as Wham!, Spandau Ballet, U2, Dire Straits, Duran Duran, and The Police. Even Beatles member Paul McCartney made an appearance. The record sold over 3 million copies in the UK alone. In 2004, a new version was made featuring Dizzee Rascal, Joss Stone, and Robbie Williams.

American idols

Following the success of *Do They Know It's Christmas?*, a group of American stars got together and made their own charity record to help starving Africans. The song they chose was called *We Are the World*. It was written by Michael Jackson and Lionel Richie and sung by an all-star cast including Stevie Wonder, Billy Joel, Bob Dylan, and Kenny Rogers.

Concert success

On 13th July 1985, many of the biggest pop stars in the world performed at the Live Aid concert at Wembley Stadium in London and at JFK Stadium in Philadelphia. The following day, the organisers announced that the concerts had raised over £50 million for charity. In 2005, two more massive concerts took place in London and Philadelphia under the name Live 8, this time featuring some of today's biggest stars.

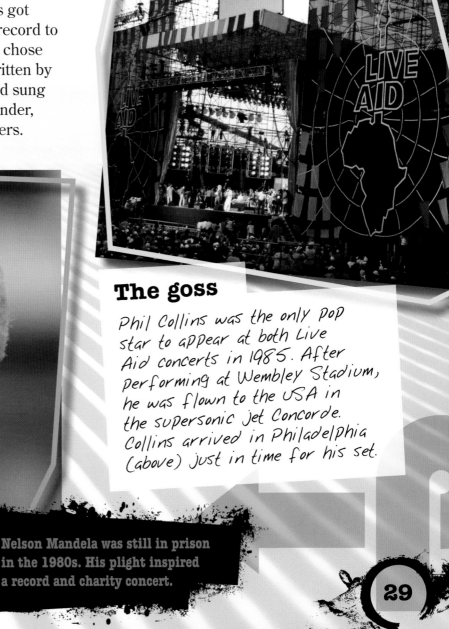

The goss

Phil Collins was the only pop star to appear at both Live Aid concerts in 1985. After performing at Wembley Stadium, he was flown to the USA in the supersonic jet Concorde. Collins arrived in Philadelphia (above) just in time for his set.

Nelson Mandela was still in prison in the 1980s. His plight inspired a record and charity concert.

HOUSE HITS

Rock and pop weren't the only styles of music undergoing massive changes in the 1980s. Dance music also had a revolution – one that continues to influence dance stars of today such as David Guetta, Fedde Le Grand, and Tiesto.

Dance music pioneer Kevin Saunderson is still part of the techno scene to this day.

Future sounds

In the summer of 1981 in Detroit, USA, a trio of high school friends began making their own electronic music at home. Using cheap synthesisers and drum machines, the trio of Juan Atkins, Derrick May, and Kevin Saunderson developed a futuristic electronic sound. Locals dubbed them 'The Belleville Three' and by 1985, they had created a brand new dance music – techno.

Warehouse music

Meanwhile, over in Chicago, USA, a trio of DJs was gaining a local reputation for using drum machines in their disco, hip-hop and electro sets. At the Warehouse, Music Box and Power Plant nightclubs, Ron Hardy, Lil' Louis, and Frankie Knuckles were laying the foundations for Chicago's own form of dance music – house.

House Trax

It wasn't long before these exciting new forms of electronic dance music from Chicago and Detroit started to get noticed across the USA

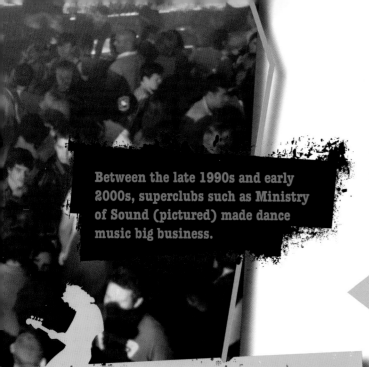

Between the late 1990s and early 2000s, superclubs such as Ministry of Sound (pictured) made dance music big business.

Under a groove

By the end of the decade, many variations of dance music had developed. Even rock bands were being influenced by dance music, with Manchester groups Happy Mondays and The Stone Roses at the centre of a world famous dance-rock fusion scene.

The goss

The first house record to hit number one in the British pop charts was Jack Your Body by Chicago producer Steve 'Silk' Hurley. It reached the top spot in January 1987 and kick-started the UK's love of house music.

The first house record

In 1984, a teenager called Jesse Saunders made a ten-minute electronic dance track in his bedroom called On and On. It was played regularly by Chicago's most important DJs. It is now widely thought of as being the first ever house record.

Dance domination

New forms of dance music inspired by house and techno went on to dominate the pop charts for the early part of the 1990s and beyond. Much of today's dance music is still based on house and techno.

and in the UK. Upon hearing the releases of pioneering record labels such as Trax, DJ International, Metroplex, and Transmat, record buyers in the USA and the UK began to pick up on house and techno.

Rave on

The rise in house music made leading British nightclubs world famous. Dancers flocked to such clubs as Manchester's Hacienda and London's Heaven. Massive outdoor 'raves' became popular with teenagers and young people, many of whom took an illegal new drug called Ecstasy. The British government was worried about the effects of Ecstasy and outdoor 'raves', and drew up laws to ban them.

Rock bands such as Happy Mondays were inspired by club culture and their music had strong dance rhythms. They even employed a dancing 'mascot' called Bez (above).

31

CHAPTER FOUR

POP WILL EAT ITSELF

Since the success of *Rapper's Delight* in 1979, hip-hop music has been on the fast-track to worldwide domination. Today, rap and R&B music rule the radio airwaves and pop charts. How did this happen?

East to West

Hip-hop pioneers such as Grandmaster Flash and the Furious Five, Kurtis Blow, Afrika Bambaataa, and KRS-One created an initial interest in rap music. This interest spread across the USA, and later the world, in the early 1980s.

Public Enemy's angry records showed that rap songs could tackle difficult subjects, such as the lives of poor black teenagers.

New styles of rap music developed, with groups such as Public Enemy, Gang Starr, and N.W.A. using the music as a way of expressing their anger about the world around them, particularly life in the poor inner-city areas.

Boys in the hood

In 1986, a former punk-rock group called The Beastie Boys scored a hit with their rock-rap single *Fight for Your Right (to Party)*. The record that followed, *Licensed to Ill*, became the number one first rap album in the USA. Thanks to the efforts of The Beastie Boys and acts such as Run D.M.C., teenagers from white, black and Latino communities could identify with hip-hop music. Sales of rap records soared.

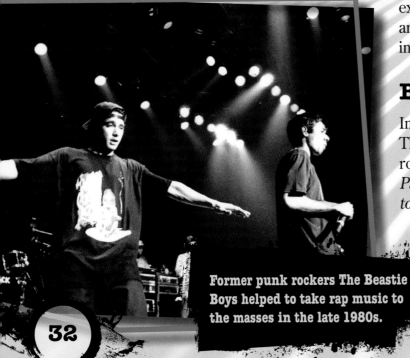

Former punk rockers The Beastie Boys helped to take rap music to the masses in the late 1980s.

The goss

In the 1980s, clothes manufacturers spotted the potential to sell sportswear through rap acts. In 1986, Run D.M.C. signed a US$18 million deal to advertise Adidas shoes and clothes. It was the first of many big money deals between rappers and clothing brands.

Worldwide success

Since the 1990s, hip-hop has become one of the most popular styles of music around the world. There are rap scenes in many countries, each with their own distinct sound, from the UK, France, and Germany to Australia, New Zealand, and Japan. Meanwhile, hip-hop beats and production styles have influenced other types of music, from indie-rock to house and dance.

Going underground

Not everyone in the hip-hop community has enjoyed the music's mainstream success in recent years. Some rap artists and fans do not regard many of the world's biggest rap hits as true hip-hop records. As a result, a strong 'underground hip-hop' scene has developed for those who want to stay true to the music's roots.

The popularity of breakdancing has increased as hip-hop has become a global musical force.

Culture club

In the 1980s and 1990s, hip-hop appealed to teenagers. Not only was the music exciting and fresh, but there was also a whole culture they could buy into. Hip-hop was just as much about the clothes you wore and the quality of your breakdancing moves as it was about music.

Superstars

In the last 20 years, many rappers have become global stars. Backed by expensive music videos that were played over and over again on television, artists such as Eminem, Jay-Z, Busta Rhymes, Nas, P. Diddy, Lil' Wayne, 50 Cent, Kanye West, and The Black Eyed Peas have sold huge amounts of records and become multimillionaires.

SUPERSTAR DJS

In the late 1990s and early 2000s, the dance music revolution started by Chicago and Detroit's producers became a massive global industry. For a brief period, a handful of DJs became the new rock stars.

Club weekends

From the late 1980s, dance music grew in popularity around the world. The number of people going to nightclubs increased, and nightclubs became the focus of many peoples' weekends. As a result, DJs responded to the demand by making their own music. They became known as musical artists in their own right – entertainers who could create an atmosphere through the blend of music they played.

Club to the studio

Many DJs with very little musical training used a combination of home computers and new music-making software to create their own dancefloor hits. DJ-producers such as Norman Cook (better known as Fatboy Slim), Orbital, Masters at Work, The Chemical Brothers, and Daft Punk became stars in their own right. People bought their records, attended their club performances and snapped up tickets for their headline appearances at dance music festivals.

Fatboy Slim is a pioneer of the big beat genre of dance music typically driven by heavy breakbeats.

Superclubs!

In the 1990s, a number of big new 'superclubs' were built to cater for the public's increased interest in dance music. Venues such as Cream in Liverpool, Gatecrasher in Sheffield, Zouk in Singapore, and Twilo in New York City booked the biggest DJs in the world and became 'must visit' destinations.

The Chemical Brothers were one of the first DJ-producers to tour the world like a rock band.

Big money

A small group of DJs became very rich indeed. The likes of Carl Cox, Paul van Dyk, and Tïesto could earn large sums for a two-hour DJ set. Some earned more in a weekend than many people could earn in a whole year. Sasha was once reportedly offered over £50,000 to play a gig on New Year's Eve, but turned it down.

Back to the underground

By 2005, a backlash had started against 'superstar DJ' culture. A new generation of teenagers was more inspired by underground, alternative rock music and hip-hop. The dance music industry suffered and returned to its underground roots. Since then, new headline DJs have appeared but they are nowhere near as popular as the 'superstar DJs' of the 1990s and 2000s.

Lasting legacy

The rise of the DJ and dance music culture in the past 30 years has left lasting marks on modern music. Without pioneers such as Sasha, Norman Cook, and Paul Oakenfold,

today's top DJ-producers would not be able to earn such a good living. Now, 'headline' DJs such as David Guetta, Armin van Buuren, and Tïesto are treated like rock stars. There may be fewer superstars than there were ten years ago, but DJs are as important to music as ever.

The goss

In July 2002, Norman Cook played a free DJ set on the beach of his home town in Brighton, UK. Organisers expected around 60,000 people to turn up. In the end, an estimated 250,000 people crowded onto the beach to hear his performance — a first in the history of DJing.

As the world's most popular 'superstar DJ', Tïesto was asked to play at the opening ceremony of the 2004 Olympics.

ROCK REVIVAL

Since the early 1990s, rock music has risen again in popularity. This is down to the mainstream success of alternative and indie artists, many of whom were inspired by rock's past.

Rock dinosaurs

At the tail end of the 1980s, rock was seen as old-fashioned. Crossover dance records and the 'manufactured' pop artists such as New Kids on the Block and Kylie Minogue dominated the airwaves.

Nirvana's grunge rock sound and tatty clothes transformed rock music and fashion in the 1990s.

Youth movement

New sound came in the form of grunge, a style of alternative rock that grew up around the American city of Seattle. Featuring distorted guitar sounds, raw music and lyrics that dealt with the more depressing side of teenage life, the music of grunge bands such as Soundgarden, Pearl Jam, Alice in Chains, and Sonic Youth hit a raw nerve with young people around the world.

Shift to mainstream

The album that marked grunge's movement into mainstream music was *Nevermind* by Seattle band Nirvana. Hailed as a rock masterpiece by critics, it replaced Michael Jackson's *Dangerous* at the top of the American album charts in 1991.

Reinventing rock

Many grunge bands were inspired by 1960s garage rock and hardcore punk. Across the other side of the Atlantic in the UK, a new wave of bands arrived with a different set of influences. They were more inspired by classic British music of the 1960s.

Cool Britannia

Influenced by bands as diverse as The Beatles, The Kinks, The Rolling Stones, and The Small Faces, 1990s 'Britpop' bands such as Blur, Oasis, Pulp, and Ocean Colour Scene had huge success with their reinventions of classic 1960s rock. American music magazines hailed the influence of these bands as a 'second British invasion', mirroring the impact of The Beatles in the 1960s.

The goss

In the summer of 1995, Blur and Oasis began a conflict known as the 'Battle of BritPop'. The bitter rivals released new singles on the same day in a bid to get one over on the other. In the end, Blur won as their song Country House hit the number one spot with Oasis' Roll With It coming in second place.

New and old

Since the end of Britpop in the early 2000s, many other forms of alternative rock music have flourished. American new-punk bands like Blink-182 and Green Day have enjoyed enormous global success, whilst Rage Against the Machine and Red Hot Chili Peppers have had success by including influences from funk and classic hip-hop.

After punk

In recent years, many bands on both sides of the Atlantic have successfully reinvented a less well-known type of music from New York called post-punk. This early 1980s original fused punk with sounds of the city's dance music scene. Today, bands such as LCD Soundsystem, The Rapture, and The Futureheads successfully combine the same musical elements.

British bands Blur (above) and Oasis (below) fought out a bitter battle for chart supremacy in 1995.

MAKING ARTISTS

Ever since the days of modern music, popular music has had its fair share of manufactured stars and hit factories. In recent years, big record labels have used television shows to get the public to join in the hit-making process and choose their own pop stars.

The X Factor has been a massive television ratings smash on both sides of the Atlantic.

Hit factories

The term 'manufactured pop' is often used to describe bands or artists whose careers are controlled by big record labels. While these artists may be talented singers or dancers, they are usually unknown artists given a chance to showcase their skills. Management companies or record company executives take them on for their look and potential appeal to music buyers.

The money men

Two men who have great experience of creating successful manufactured pop bands are Simon Fuller and Simon Cowell. These British businessmen were behind some of the biggest pop acts of the 1990s, including The Spice Girls and Westlife.

Popstars

Fuller and Cowell used a television show called *Popstars* to put together a new manufactured pop band. Viewers voted for their favourite contestants until a band was created. The winners – Hear'Say – were given the prize of a recording contract.

Ratings success

Fuller and Cowell's idea was a massive ratings success. A number of other shows followed the same successful idea, including *Pop Idol*, *American Idol*, *Britain's Got Talent*, *America's Got Talent*, and *The X Factor*. In most cases, the winner's debut single has hit the top spot in the American or British charts.

Not a fan...

Not all music fans enjoy these reality television shows and their effect on popular music. In 2009, a campaign was organised on the Internet to prevent that year's *X Factor* single securing the prized Christmas number one slot in the British pop charts.

Global icons

Although only a very small number of today's music stars started their careers by appearing on television reality shows, they have helped to create a number of genuine pop stars. These include British singers Leona Lewis and Susan Boyle, and American artists Kelly Clarkson and Carrie Underwood.

Buying in the name

The campaign was hugely popular with fans of alternative and underground music. They hated the sort of manufactured pop produced by Cowell's *X Factor* and *Got Talent* shows. Many bands and musicians supported the campaign, and Rage Against the Machine's rock anthem *Killing in the Name* sold enough copies to send it to the top of the charts. The band donated all the profits from sales to charity.

The goss

Susan Boyle (above) became a worldwide sensation after appearing on Britain's Got Talent in 2009. Within a week of her first performance on the show, clips of her appearance had been viewed over 100 million times on YouTube. Her first record went on to become the biggest-selling debut album in British chart history.

Kelly Clarkson was one of the first reality TV contestants to become a global pop sensation.

The iPod

In the last decade, the way people buy and listen to music has changed hugely. Now, we can find, buy and listen to music on mobile phones, tablets and many other portable devices. This change was kick-started by a revolutionary product – the iPod.

The success of the iPod has changed the way we buy, listen to and share music.

MP3 magic

In 1998, software developers in the USA announced that they'd come up with a new way of storing music on computers – MP3 files. These were small and took up very little space on a computer's hard drive, meaning that PC and Mac users could easily build up huge libraries of songs. A number of electronics companies decided to launch portable MP3 players that were capable of storing a small selection of songs. They proved popular with hardcore computer users but did not sell in big numbers.

Faster Internet

Computer users began to see the potential of MP3 files when faster Internet connections arrived in around 2000. Now, they could easily download small music MP3 files from specialist websites.

Digital pirates

The music industry reacted strongly to what it called 'Internet piracy'. They were particularly annoyed by Napster, a service that allowed people to swap digital music files for free. Suddenly, any track became free of charge.

Steve Jobs' vision

Apple Computer co-founder Steve Jobs saw the potential of MP3s and the Internet as a way of distributing and selling music. He wanted to create a portable music player that could store large amounts of music. He thought there would be a market for a device that could hold around 1,000 songs.

iPod is a hit

Steve Jobs was proved right. Apple launched the iPod digital music player in September 2001 and it was an immediate success. Despite being quite expensive, sales were quick.

Goodbye CDs

By 2003, Jobs was ready to launch the next phase of his plan, the iTunes Store. This innovation allowed iPod users to legally buy music files and download them directly to their iPod devices. Users would be able to buy individual songs if they wished, as well as whole albums. For the first time, music fans could pick and choose what they wanted to buy and listen to – they no longer had to buy a whole CD to get the one track they wanted.

iPod mania

At the same time as the iTunes store launched, Apple announced a new range of iPods that could be used with PC computers. Sales of iPods soared and soon more people were buying music downloads than CDs. To date, nearly 300 million iPods have been sold worldwide.

The late Steve Jobs' 'big idea' has made Apple one of the richest companies in the world.

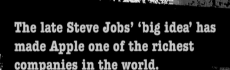

TIMELINE: The iPod

1998: The first widely-available portable MP3 player, the MPMan, is launched
2001: Apple launches the first iPod with a capacity of 1,000 songs
2003: iTunes Music Store launches

2007: Apple launches the iPhone, a mobile telephone and iPod combined
2010: Apple announces it has sold over 275 million iPods since 2001
2011: iTunes Store sells its 1 th billionth song

POWER TO THE PEOPLE

Since rock and roll shook the music industry to its foundations in the 1950s, popular music has changed beyond recognition. Thanks to the Internet and other advances in technology, music fans and bedroom producers are shaping the future of music.

Closed shop

Less than 30 years ago, music was controlled by a small group of major record labels, a handful of music magazines and a string of popular radio stations. Labels carefully chose the releases, journalists wrote about them and radio stations played the music. Mainstream music fans had little choice about what they listened to.

Computer music

Things began to change in the 1990s when computers became more affordable and powerful. Suddenly, software became available that allowed enthusiastic young musicians to make their own music. They didn't need to spend money on hiring out record studios – they could do it all in their bedrooms.

Download this!

The Internet changed everything. Music could now easily be distributed around the world as MP3 files. There was no need to buy CDs or vinyl records when you could spend a few pence on a brand new song, or download one for free.

Apple's iTunes Store sold its 16th billionth song in October 2011, just eight years after it was launched.

The goss

Several teenage musicians have achieved big record contracts after posting their tracks on video sharing website YouTube. Alyssa Bernal was signed to Star Trak Records in 2010 after global soul star Pharrell Williams watched one of her videos on the Internet.

Social upheaval

The Internet has made it easier for young musicians to get their songs heard by many more people, and for new trends to quickly develop. Now, you could make a track in an evening, upload it to the Internet and get feedback in minutes.

No more record labels

The Internet has also allowed musicians to bypass record labels. Now, bands can sell their songs through websites such as Bandcamp. Some big artists, such as Radiohead, have even experimented with giving away their music to fans for free.

Online services such as Spotify and YouTube make it easy to listen to whatever you want, whenever you want.

The Internet music revolution has allowed bands such as Radiohead to sell or give away their music directly to fans.

World music

All these changes in technology and communication mean that previously tiny local trends and musical styles can spread around the world in weeks, days or hours. For example, in 2011 British clubs went mad for the sounds of Juke and Footstep, two obscure forms of dance music made in Chicago. Instrumental hip-hop changed dramatically in 2010 and 2011, too, thanks to the experimental production techniques of artists variously based in Los Angeles, Scotland, and Portugal.

Global groove

It is now possible for bedroom musicians to build up a huge following around the world without spending a single penny. What's more, music fans now have more choice than ever before. New forms of music can take hold on the Internet in days or weeks, and then change within a few months. All this has made the world of modern music more exciting than ever. We've never had it so good!

GLOSSARY

acoustic non-electric instruments, for example a traditional acoustic guitar

alternative rockers people who make or listen to alternative or underground rock music

assassination term used to describe the murder of a high profile figure such as a president, politician or head of state

backing track the music over which an MC 'raps' or a singer sings

bass line a sequence of low, deep musical notes often used as part of a song's backing track. The bass line helps to give the song rhythm and momentum

block parties outdoor, often illegal, music and dance events held in local parks and other open spaces

Bronx a poor, run-down area of New York City

chords groups of musical notes played at the same time

credited to to say someone is responsible for making something, for example a record

dance-rock fusion music that uses elements of both traditional rock and electronic dance music

digital sampler an electronic machine used to record – 'sample' – and edit sounds or short excerpts from recordings

distorted guitar sounds strange and fuzzy sounds made using an electric guitar and a special effects unit

distributing the process of getting a product – for example, a record – to shops

editing the process of cutting and re-arranging pre-recorded music or film, using tape or, nowadays, computer software

experimental trying to do things in new, different and unconventional ways

folk a traditional form of music that developed over hundreds of years

funk a heavy form of dance music that originated in black American communities in the late 1960s and early 1970s

fuse join together

futuristic something that looks or sounds like it comes from the future

garage rock a loose and noisy form of rock music that has its origins in the bedrooms and garages of 1960s America

gospel singing a form of religious music traditionally sung by black people in church

hit factories recording studios that specialise in making hit pop records

horn musical slang for brass instruments such as trumpet, trombone and saxophone

iconic a moment or person that goes down in history

jazz an inventive style of music created by black musicians using traditional instruments such as saxophone, trumpet, drums and piano

Latin music influenced by the sounds of South America, such as samba and mambo

Latino term used to refer to Americans whose families originally came from central and South American countries such as Puerto Rico and Brazil

looping techniques the process of repeating a pre-recorded sound or musical section using a tape machine or computer program

LSD an illegal drug that causes people to view the world in a strange way and can cause serious brain damage

mainstream popular with a lot of people

management companies firms who specialise in 'managing' the affairs of music, television or film stars, for example negotiating contracts and coming up with strategies to make them more famous

manufactured pop music designed to appeal to a particular group of people, or to as many different people as possible

mind-altering drugs or substances that change the way people view the world

pioneers people who do something first

production styles methods of making, recording and 'producing' music

psychedelic term used to refer to the effects of certain illegal drugs, such as LSD, and music made by people who experimented with those drugs

'quick mix' mixing the process of quickly alternating between music stored on vinyl records played on two different turntables

race laws strict laws in the USA that meant that black people didn't have the same rights as white people

racist system racism against black people built into the way a country is run

record company executives people who manage big record labels – companies who specialise in selling music

record producer a person who specialises in recording and producing music

revolutionary an action that is so different and monumental that it changes the way people think, do something or live their lives

rhythm and blues a popular form of music made using guitars and drums that was originally invented by black musicians

supersonic faster than the speed of sound

trademark sound the musical style of a band, singer or record label that listeners can identify them by (for example, the Motown soul sound)

underground less well-known

Vietnam War a long-running and unpopular war in Vietnam, Asia (1955–1975). American armed forces joined the conflict in 1965

FURTHER READING

Books

Jeremy J Beadle: *Will Pop Eat Itself? Pop Music in the Soundbite Era* (Faber & Faber, 1993)

Bill Brewster & Frank Broughton: *Last Night a DJ Saved My Life – 100 Years of the Disc Jockey* (Headline, 2006)

Melanie J Cornish: *The Story of Hip-Hop* (TickTock Books, 2009)

Nelson George: *Where Did Our Love Go? The Rise and Fall of the Motown Sound* (Omnibus Press, 2003)

Websites

Listen to Radio One's online story of the music industry at:
www.radiolistings.co.uk/programmes/ s/st/story_of_pop__the.html

Take a tour of modern pop music at:
www.popproject.co.uk

Read stories about the history of pop at:
www.pophistorydig.com

Note to parents and teachers
Every effort has been made by the Publisher to ensure that these websites contain no inappropriate or offensive material. However, because of the nature of the Internet, it is impossible to guarantee that the contents of these sites will not be altered. We strongly advise that Internet access is supervised by a responsible adult.

INDEX